OPTIONS TRADING

— — — — — ❧ ❦❧❦❧ — — — —

A Crash Course to Quickly Set Up and Make Instant Cash with Stock Options

Anthony Kreil

liable for any hardship or damages that may befall them after undertaking information described herein.

Additionally, the information in the following pages is intended only for informational purposes and should thus be thought of as universal. As befitting its nature, it is presented without assurance regarding its prolonged validity or interim quality. Trademarks that are mentioned are done without written consent and can in no way be considered an endorsement from the trademark holder.

DISCLAIMER

Although the author and publisher have made every effort to ensure that the information in this book was correct at press time, the author and publisher do not assume and hereby disclaim any liability to any party for any loss, damage, or disruption caused by errors or omissions, whether such errors or omissions result from negligence, accident, or any other cause.

Table of Contents

Introduction

Congratulations on downloading this book and thank you for doing so.

The following chapters will discuss how to quickly set up an options trading account so you can begin trading and making money as soon as possible. While trading may not be as easy as it may sound, there are plenty of simple techniques that you can learn and apply. If properly applied, then you can begin to grow your account and get attractive returns.

There is a huge difference between investing, trading individual stock market instruments, and trading options. Options trading is by far the most lucrative alternative. It is also less risky because you do not have to spend your resources buying stocks. Some of the wealthiest individuals at the stock markets are actually options traders.

There are plenty of books on this subject on the market, so thanks again for choosing this one! Every effort was made to ensure it is full of as much useful information as possible. Please enjoy!

Chapter 1:
Essentials of Options Trading

O ptions trading is arguably more complex compared to stock trading. This is because options are derivatives of other securities. Without these other securities, such as stocks, bonds, indexes, currencies, and so on, options would not exist. It is crucial that you also understand the basics. By understanding as much as you can about options trading, you will be able to confidently trade and build your account progressively.

A Summary of the Options Trading Process

By now, you already know that an option is basically a contract that awards you the right to purchase or sell a security at a given price. However, options are always time-specific. There is a time limit as to how long your rights to buy or sell the security last. This time could range from a number of days to even weeks or months. An important distinction about options is that you are not obliged to exercise your right to buy or sell the underlying security.

Call and Put Options

We can divide options into two basic categories. These are Call options and Put options. A call option is an option that comes with a right to purchase an underlying asset within a certain time frame. Remember that all options are based on a certain security. On the other hand, a put option is the reverse of the call option. A put option gives you the right—but not the obligation—to sell an asset within a given time period.

With call options, you buy the option simply because you believe its price will go up within the time frame given. This way, you will be buying it at a cheaper price with the hope of selling at a better price in the near future. With put options, you have the right to sell a security. You would mostly sell if you believe the price will go down at a later date.

Important Terms Associated with Options Trading

There are certain basic terms that you need to learn about trading options. While these terms are basic, they are crucial if you are to trade successfully. Here is a look at these crucial terms.

Strike price: Whenever you buy or sell an option, you will do so based on the price indicated. This set price is what is referred to as the strike price.

Term: You can exercise your right to sell or buy the underlying security of an option within a certain time frame. This time frame, which ranges from a day to a couple of months, is known as the term.

Market price: The price at which an underlying security will fetch at the market is known as the market price. It is sometimes higher and other times lower than the strike price.

Exchange: Options are bought or sold on a platform known as the options exchange. The main challenge that causes options to be so risky is the time frame or term limit.

The Actual Trading of Options

Options can be traded in either of two ways. You can purchase options to hedge against possible losses or for speculative purposes. When you purchase options for hedging purposes, then you do so to prevent a possible loss that you or an organization are likely to experience.

When it comes to speculation, you will trade options with the hope of making large amounts of money. This is possible only if you are able to accurately predict the direction, timing, and magnitude of the price movement of the underlying stock. It is this speculative nature of options that introduces the risk element. However, with the correct risk mitigation techniques, you are able to minimize your losses and greatly improve your chances of success.

Find and Read the Booklet about the Risks and Characteristics of Options

There is a booklet that has been written about the characteristics and risks involved in trading standardized options. This book has been written in tandem with the regulations provided and with compliance to SEC or Securities and Exchange Commission. The main aim of the book is to move you away from the theory that you learn about options. Instead, it will wake you up to the realistic aspects of trading options.

They are rife with risks especially if you do not take charge of stop-loss measures. As a trader, you need to learn all about risk management in order to ensure that your trades are profitable and any risks incurred are minimal. Also, remember that there is no trader who does not lose some money. Everyone loses some money in trading, even the seasoned experts. Therefore, learn how to minimize losses, ensure that you know how to perform technical analysis and how to read charts. This way, you should be safe and protected as you trade.

Most brokerage firms are in possession of this booklet. They will gladly let you have a copy. Ensure that you read and understand it. The booklet will teach all about the essential terminology, how to exercise and also settle options, different types of options that you can deal in, risks associated with such trades and all the tax considerations.

You Need to Understand Basic Trading

As we have already noted earlier, there are essentially two different types of options. These are the call options and put options. These two options types give you a right to either sell or purchase an underlying security at a set price and within a set period of time. A trader who buys a call option is of the opinion that the price of the underlying security will rise within the prescribed period of time.

Let us look at a real-time call option example.

A trader buys a call option whose underlying stock has a strike price of $150. The trader is of the opinion that the price will rise to $160 within the prescribed time. However, he is able to purchase the stocks at $150. After the price goes up as predicted, he will be able to sell the stocks at the new price. This will earn him a profit of about $10 * 100 = $1000. If this does not work out, then the trader will lose the money paid for the option which is often not more than $2 per share.

Open an Options Trading Account

Now once you are ready to apply your skills and techniques, you should then identify a reliable broker and open a trading account. There are plenty of brokers out there so be careful to find a reliable and trustworthy one. The reason you need a broker is so that you can be hooked up or connected to the trading platform. There are good examples of reliable brokers online so take your time to identify the most trustworthy and reliable.

You can also use a brokerage firm instead of the traditional broker account. There are a couple of trustworthy sites that provide brokerage services including the site www.iqoptionsbid.com. There are quite a number of things involved in opening an account so be sure to address all the requirements. Also, there are a few things you need to be on the lookout for. These are listed below.

You need to compare the commissions charged by different brokers and brokerage firms. There are some with excellent rules, others do not charge commissions, while others are quite costly and demanding,

Try and read up online about any prospective brokerage firms that you want to join. Also, read and research as much information about your potential broker. How do other traders rate the broker? Does he or she have a good reputation? It is always advisable to learn from other people's mistakes so you do not repeat them yourself.

Be very careful about scammers, phishing sites, and other unscrupulous people out there. Many of them pretend to be genuine brokers or brokerage firms but they are really out there to rip you off. Do not deposit any money into an account even after you open one. Be cautious, take your time, and be sure.

Only then after everything adds up should you then think about depositing some money. Websites with reported cases of fraud or negative reviews should be avoided at all costs.

There is a cash account and then there is a margin account. You will need a cash account if you want to only buy options and then enter a position. However, if you intend to actually enter a position and hold, you will need a margin account.

Another factor that you need to consider is the different forms of payment available. It is recommended that you find a trading account that accepts a variety of payments ranging from bitcoin to Skrill, Payoneer, and even PayPal. Also important are accounts that can accept most major credit cards. Secure credit card payments are crucial for most accounts.

Seek the Necessary Approvals

Now, as soon as your account is up and running, you will have to fund it. These funds will be used to enter different trades even as you seek to trade, sell, or buy and become profitable.

However, you will need to get approved. The brokerage house that you engage will have to approve you. They will base the approval on a couple of factors such as your location, amount of funds available to trade, and similar things. Also, each brokerage firm has its own list of requirements so you will need to meet these requirements as well.

The brokerage firms also need to be sure that you really know what it is that you are doing and that you understand the risks associated with stocks trading.

Ensure that you Understand Technical Analysis

One of the most crucial steps that you need to be conversant with is technical analysis. The information and data that is derived from a proper technical analysis will enable you to profit. Basically, options are considered to be a short-term investment and this means you should find price movements of underlying securities in the immediate future in order to profit from the trade. The following are some useful points that will guide you to properly predict price movements. These will form the basis of any technical analysis you will need.

1. Learn about resistance and support levels

It is crucial that you learn and understand all about support and resistance levels as pertaining to stocks and options. These are actual points where the stock will not rise above (resistance) or fall below (support).

Basically, we identify support levels as the level where substantial buying has occurred in the past. On the other hand, we can identify points of resistance as price levels where significant levels of stock sales occurred. These points are best identified using technical analysis. Now, research has shown stock market behavior is almost similar through the years. This means that we can accurately use past data to deduce or predict future events.

2. Understand Volume Trading

You need to understand the benefit and importance of volume in trading. As a trader, only handle securities that have sufficient volumes. This is because volumes are a pointer to liquidity. Stocks that have little or no volume that is considered sufficient for the stock market trading should not be traded. Also, anytime the stock is headed in a particular direction and volumes are high, then the trend is likely to be strong. This is a pointer at a chance for making money.

3. Learn about Chart Patterns

You should also ensure that you understand chart patterns very well. Charts are meant to help you with your technical analysis. Like we have said before, history tends to repeat itself. Chart patterns are, therefore, crucial at determining the indicative performance of the markets.

4. Don't forget the Moving Averages

Another important parameter you need to learn about is the moving average. There are a couple of different moving averages. They include the 10-day moving average and the

30-day moving average. It is often the case that when the price of a stock crosses above or below one of these moving averages that direction changes.

Begin Simulator Trading

Now that you have learned all the essential theories, the next step is to put all this knowledge into practice. You can start by paper trading or even use a simulator. It is important that you avoid the temptation of using your own funds to trade. At this juncture, it would be too risky to use your own money. Options trading is still a risky practice, especially for beginners.

You should first enter pretend trends and use a piece of paper and pen. Let us see how you perform with these. The crucial area of concern at this juncture is to see if you can apply all that you have learned. You can, for instance, enter trades on a spreadsheet and see if you can perform technical analysis and also come up with all the crucial indicators.

It is evident that paper trading is different from actual trading. However, the experience is vital if you are to eventually trade options at the options markets. Paper trading is great for the mechanical aspect of trading. You get to understand exactly how things work in reality. However, it cannot help you to predict real results. When you eventually begin trading, you should do so only with money that you can afford to lose but not money meant for living expenses.

Loss Management Techniques

You should always enter the markets with a sure loss management process in place. This way, you will be able to limit your losses and keep them to a minimum. For instance, make use of limit orders as a stop-loss measure. You should not pay market price when trading options because there are other costs involved such as the execution costs. You instead choose to name a price and use limit orders in order to maximize your returns.

Always re-evaluate your trading strategy. Re-evaluation is an important practice that should be undertaken periodically. When re-evaluating the strategy, try and see if there is anything you can improve on. If you have been making some mistakes, then you should learn from them. Also, focus on only a couple of positions. Most traders often focus on a few positions and never diversification. Ideally, you should not have more than 10 different portfolio items.

Other Tips and Advice

Think about joining a forum of advanced traders. There are plenty of such forums online. By joining such a platform, you will get insightful knowledge, support when you suffer losses, and also a chance to share with people with similar interests to yours. With time, you should also try and move to advanced options trading. Rather than stick to just one single strategy, try and move on to another strategy. This way, you will be able to apply more advanced techniques that are likely to earn you a higher income. You can learn about these techniques on various online platforms where like-minded experts regularly visit and comment.

Chapter 2:
How to Open a Stock Trading Account

Opening a stock trading account is a straightforward process. However, before you can embark on the process, your broker will need a little more information about you. For instance, the broker wants to know how much capital you have, your competence level, nationality and that kind of detail. This way, they will be able to grant you permission to begin trading options.

Basic Essentials

Even brokerage firms need a little more information about you. They seek information such as ensuring you understand the risks that you will be exposed to as well as your financial knowledge and preparedness. Brokers often assign you a competence level or trading level, depending on your stated experience.

Therefore, provide your broker or brokerage firm with the following information:

- Your trading experience and investment knowledge

- Your overall investment objectives such as income, wealth generation, etc.

- Your personal information, especially financial information like net worth

- Provide information on the kind of options you wish to trade

This kind of information is crucial so that you are awarded the appropriate trading level. You need to choose your broker carefully because they will be among your most important partner in your trading journey. So, just as the broker screens you, you also need to screen them too. Screening a broker is part of your due diligence. If you do not follow this crucial step, then it may come back to haunt you in future.

There are a couple of questions that you need to ask before choosing a broker. Some traders search for one who charges the cheapest commissions while others search for a broker with the best customer service or trading tools. Others consider platform design and others all the above. Even online reputation is also considered. Basically, a suitable broker is one with a robust platform and the following features:

- No account minimum
- Low commissions
- Robust research tools
- A reliable web-based platform
- Free research

Then there are some things you would want to avoid in a broker. Some of these include:

- High, short-term ETF trading fee
- Expensive broker-aided trades
- Costly trade commissions
- No commission-free ETFs

You can search or find help to determine how you compare minimums, costs, and other features. It is crucial that you find the most appropriate and most suitable broker. This is because your success will depend on your broker to a large extent.

To find a suitable broker, there are some questions that you need to answer. It is the answers that will guide you towards your preferred broker. Here are a couple of screener questions.

- How much do you intend to deposit into your account as trading capital? Is it less than $2,500, between $2,500 and $5,000 or greater than $5,000?

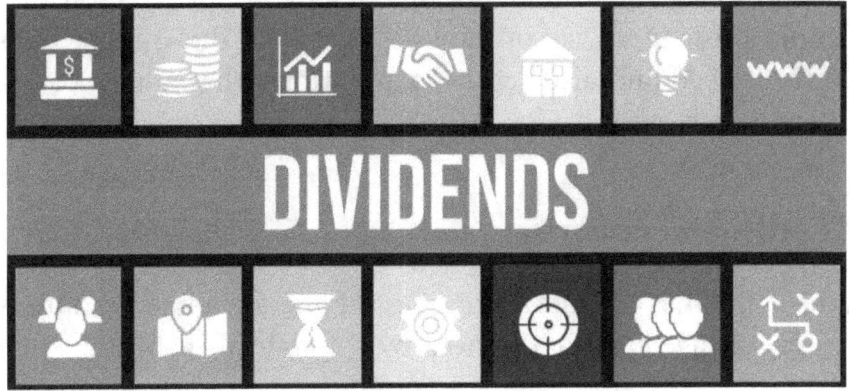

Select an Online Broker

It is important to consider tools offered by a broker and the fees he charges. These two considerations are of paramount importance. If you are a beginner or novice trader, then you will want to find a broker who offers excellent customer service because you will definitely need some assistance along the way.

At this stage, you probably won't find brokers that charge low fees. Basically, you should aim to pay no more than $4 to $10 per trade. You probably won't trade much as a beginner and novice trader. Once your skills get better and you start trading more often, then you can consider moving to a more affordable broker.

Also, take a look at your broker's software. This software should be easy to navigate and also streamlined. A good platform that is presentable, easy to navigate, and user-friendly is what you should be on the lookout for. The software should provide advice on how to access all the trading tools you will need and also access to a platform that allows you to interact with other traders.

Trading Accounts

When it comes to trade and investments, a trading account is simply an account that is held by a financial institution that you open as a trader. These accounts are not normally opened directly but via a broker or investment dealer. The account is for you and is meant for your trading and investment purposes. It can hold all sorts of securities from stocks to currencies, bonds, and numerous others.

The best way to fund your account is via your bank account. This will establish and confirm your identity. It will also prove that the funds belong to you. You cannot use a check issued by a friend to fund your account.

Margin Trading Account

You can choose between opening a margin trading account or a cash account. A margin trading account comes with a credit line directly from your broker. This credit line makes it possible for you to purchase stocks, options, and other types of securities whenever you wish. You also get the chance to buy options directly.

Cash Trading Account

This type of trading account allows you to enter trades using only the cash in your account. Basically, you have $5,000 in your account then you can only use the $5,000 for your trades. You will also be required to close one position before acquiring more purchase power.

Since this is a cash account, you are generally not permitted to borrow any cash. The good news is that any cash settlements are often processed within a day. Let us assume you transact today. Any cash settlements can be sorted out within a 24-hour period. However, this is just with some brokers and not all. There are those who take up to 3 days to process settlements.

Margin

A lot of the time, brokerage firms will offer you some margin. This is additional credit that enables you to invest in more stock. A margin account is similar to receiving a loan from an institution. This means that you will pay some interest on the cash advance. This interest is charged only if you hold a position overnight. The amount of interest charged is often 2% over and above the prevailing market rates. Remember that you will be responsible for paying back this money, regardless of whether or not you earned a profit.

Margin is often handed out to qualifying accounts at a rate of 2:1. This applies to accounts whose balance is less than $25,000. For instance, if your account balance is $15,000, then you have access to a total of $30,000 which you can use to place trades and buy into positions. Account holders with more than $25,000 can get access to credit in the ratio of 4:1. This is a lot of money so please be careful if and when you do qualify.

Your Personal Information

Even as you open your trading account, you will be required to provide some personal information. Each broker needs to receive some personal details about you. This information is crucial for purposes such as tax tracking, account management, and other reasons. In fact, a law passed by US Congress requires brokers to acquire personal information from individuals opening trading accounts. As a trader, you will be expected to provide accurate information about yourself. Your brokerage firm also requires this information should they need to get in touch with you and discuss a couple of things.

List of Personal Information a Broker is Likely to Request:

- Your full names
- Phone number
- Street address
- Social security number
- Email address
- Date of birth
- Estimated annual income
- US citizenship status
- Place of employment
- Federal tax bracket
- Any prior market experience

This information is necessary because they really need to know who it is that they are working with. Therefore, always be truthful and honest with information and save yourself unnecessary delays or trouble.

When asked about net worth, most people think it is about cash in the bank, a business, and property such as a home. However, this includes other things such as the car you own, a TV set, kitchen appliances and things like that too. Also, let them know if you have any market experience. If you have even had a 401(K) or mutual funds then you should reveal this information. It is to your disadvantage if you do not have any market experience. Please keep in mind that incorrect and inaccurate information could get you kicked off a trading platform.

Funding your Trading Account

You will need to fund your account in order to begin trading. You should consider making the first deposit through automatic transfer from your bank. Most brokerage firms provide this service during business hours. Another option is to send a check to the brokerage firm. If you are writing a personal check then you should put your name on it.

You can choose to transfer any stocks, bonds, options, and other securities that you have elsewhere to your new account. Most brokerage firms have some minimum deposit requirement. At some places, it is $500, while at others it can be well over $10,000. There are those that even request a minimum of $1 million. Sometimes, there is idle cash in your account. You may want to let your broker put this money into stocks, bonds, or mutual funds so it earns you an interest. It is better to have your money growing rather than letting it sit without earning you an interest.

Final Steps to Opening an Account

You will receive a statement from your broker when you finally open an account. This is a statement of understanding between you and your broker. It is to clear the air and help you understand exactly what he can expect from you and you from him.

You should read through the entire document and ensure that you understand each and every word written there. A lot of the information on this statement confirms that you are of legal age and that you understand exactly what you are getting into as well as the risks you will be exposed to. You should print out the document after signing and keep a copy for yourself.

How to Trade with your New Account

Now think about the core constituents of an options trade. Any options trade has to have a contract because this is what you are purchasing. The contract gives you a right—but not an obligation—to purchase or sell a stock within a certain time period. The price of the stock is usually pre-negotiated. Before buying this contract, there are a couple of things that you will need to consider.

- Determine the direction that the stock might move toward

- Consider or predict how high or how low the stock price will move

- Determine the amount of time within which the stock will move

1. Stock Direction Movement

The direction of the stock movement, whether up or down, will largely influence the type of options contract that you are going to buy. Basically, you will choose a call option if you think that the price will go up. The reason is that a call option comes with a contract that gives you rights to buy a stock at a determined price. This price is known as the strike price. There is a time limit to this contract.

If you think that the price will go down, then you should choose a put option. Remember that a put option is an options contract that gives you the right to sell a stock (but not an obligation) within the stipulated time period.

2. Predict the Stock Price Movement

The next thing you need to do is to determine the level at which the stock price will rise or drop from its current position. Remember that the option is only valid for as long as it is within its stipulated time frame. Also, the stock is valuable when the price is able to close the option expiration time "In the Money."

The term, "In the Money" simply means that the options time runs out while the stock is above the strike price for call options and below the strike price for put options. Basically, when you want to buy an option, ensure that it has a strike price which indicates the kind of price you desire within its lifetime.

Chapter 3:
How to Start Trading
with your Account

Now that your account is open and funded, you are probably ready to begin trading. However, before you begin, make sure that you understand how stocks, options, and other securities work. Ensure that you have a good trading strategy and that you have excellent loss prevention and risk management strategies.

Remember that trading individual stocks is pretty risky and needs a lot more effort compared to investment in index funds or mutual funds. However, it has also been shown that it is much more profitable to invest in stock options. The risks are minimal while the benefits are impressive.

1. Consider Learning How to Trade

You probably have little or no trading skill. If this is the case, then you should think about getting an education. Learn as much as you can about trading and investing in the markets. A single mistake can be quite costly. Therefore, avoid any unnecessary mistakes by educating yourself.

You can find plenty of educational materials or resources at your broker's platform. There is material that teaches you how to trade via the platform. There are also lessons that you can learn via www.udemy.com and Morning Star Investing Classroom. Even as you get the education, make sure that you practice trading too.

Try both paper trading exercises and use of a trade simulator. You should practice trading as often as you can. Take these exercises seriously because they resemble real-life trading. Once you are confident enough, you may then think about trading using actual money. However, before you start trading any options, do your research.

2. Begin Undertaking your Research

Now that you are ready to begin trading, what options or stocks will you be interested in? Find those that you have an interest in. For instance, do you love sports? Consider stocks in the sporting industry. You will also need to learn how to read charts, do technical analysis, and maintain discipline.

All these are essential ingredients if you are to be successful. Find a trading strategy that works for you. For instance, you can choose to trade in credit spreads only or combine that with something else. When you begin trading, make sure that you start very slowly. Choose just one option and see how it goes. If you can, then try and pick another one. See how these two trades go. At this stage, you are trying to apply your knowledge, prevent losses, and see how the trade goes.

3. Identify a Strategy and Create a Plan

It is very important that you come up with a trading plan. It is even more important to stick to any plan that you come up with. Basically, a good plan is one that is well-thought-out—one that is supported by both technical and fundamental analysis. If you are happy dealing with credit spread options or payday options, then focus on these only. Do not change your mind mid-way because this is a sure way of failure.

Ensure that you stick to your plan. All too often, young, novice traders abandon a plan midway and try to change tactics. This is not advisable at all. Your plan should be supported by your analysis. If you think a strategy is not working, then you can change it later on and try a new one.

You can always change strategies so you find one that suits you perfectly. This is definitely okay. Make sure that you use tools such as the limit orders. These orders allow you to place an order for options and then name your price. This way, you will minimize your losses and maximize your income. Do not pay market price when buying options as the prices may be higher than you would expect.

You also need to learn about risk management techniques. Options trading can be highly speculative with plenty of risks. Learning how to mitigate against these risks should be a huge part of the trading plan. Also, make a determination about how much money you are going to invest in your trades. Work out what risk management techniques you will adopt. Remember to avoid emotional interventions and let the trades flow according to your plan. Remember that you are allowed to re-evaluate your trading strategy from time to time.

This is important so that if it is not working according to plan then you can devise another one. Also, try and learn new options trading techniques in order to diversify your trades. If you need advice or assistance, then never shy away from asking. Consult your broker or seasoned traders and you will most likely receive the advice that you need.

4. Advanced Options Trading Techniques

If you eventually become good at trading options, then you may want to perform even better. To achieve this, you will need to move on to advanced options trading. Such techniques will definitely fetch you better prices at the markets and help you in diversification.

One of the best places to learn more about these techniques is on an online platform. You should try and find a platform where seasoned and new traders meet to discuss their trades. Platforms with like-minded traders will provide you with excellent ideas, comfort, and so much more. There, you will meet traders with similar thoughts and ideas as you. You will truly feel at home sharing ideas and experiences with your peers.

You should also, at this stage, consider other options trading strategies. Some of the complex ones include the Greeks. Greeks are metrics used by options traders in order to maximize their returns. Terms such as delta, gamma, and vega are common among experienced traders.

Options Trading

	1	2	3	4	5	6	7	8	9	10	11	12
	OpSym	Bid (pts)	Ask (pts)	Extrinsic Bid/Ask (pts)	IV Bid/Ask (%)	Delta Bid/Ask (%)	Gamma Bid/Ask (%)	Vega Bid/Ask (pts/% IV)	Theta Bid/Ask (pts/day)	Volume	Open Interest	Strike
	IBM MAR10 110 C	16.25	16.70	0.00 / 0.37	19.77 / 35.15	99.16 / 92.06	0.27 / 1.15	0.007 / 0.053	0.0009 / -0.0279	0	479	110.000
	IBM MAR10 115 C	11.65	11.80	0.32 / 0.47	25.37 / 27.68	90.52 / 88.67	1.82 / 1.90	0.060 / 0.069	-0.0227 / -0.0290	47	552	115.000
	IBM MAR10 120 C	7.15	7.30	0.82 / 0.97	21.85 / 23.30	79.89 / 78.51	3.53 / 3.45	0.101 / 0.105	-0.0244 / -0.0385	360	1179	120.000
	IBM MAR10 125 C	3.40	3.50	2.07 / 2.17	19.04 / 19.75	58.20 / 57.98	5.65 / 5.46	0.141 / 0.141	-0.0431 / -0.0448	1268	5782	125.000
	Stock											126.33
	IBM MAR10 130 C	1.10	1.14	1.10 / 1.14	17.41 / 17.73	28.66 / 29.04	5.40 / 5.33	0.123 / 0.124	-0.0349 / -0.0358	1868	5947	130.000
	IBM MAR10 135 C	0.23	0.25	0.23 / 0.25	16.73 / 17.08	8.45 / 8.91	2.36 / 2.61	0.056 / 0.058	-0.0154 / -0.0164	666	6539	135.000
	IBM MAR10 140 C	0.04	0.06	0.04 / 0.06	17.04 / 18.12	1.82 / 2.47	0.72 / 0.88	0.016 / 0.021	-0.0045 / -0.0062	80	4284	140.000
	IBM MAR10 145 C	0.00	0.03	0.00 / 0.03	0.00 / 21.03	0.00 / 1.17	0.00 / 0.40	0.000 / 0.011	0.0000 / -0.0038	10	1747	145.000

Chapter 4:
Make Quick Money Trading
Call Options

Now that your trading account is up and running, it is time to begin earning quick profits. You will be much better off trading options than stocks. This is because options trading is so much more profitable than just trading other securities. It is also much easier than you may think, so let us take a look at a simple call option trading situation.

Trading Call Options

One of the easiest and stress-free ways of trading options is through buying call options. Let us look at an example just to demonstrate how it works.

Let us assume that the stock YHOO is trading at $50. According to your estimation, this stock will rise in price in the next couple of weeks. You believe that it will get to $60 within that time period. There is one way of profiting from this situation and that is to purchase about $100 of the stock. If you buy it today at $50, it will cost you $5000. After a few weeks, if your assumptions were right, you could sell the same stock for $60 each and get $6000. This would result in a profit of $1000. This will amount to a 25% return on investment which is not bad at all.

However, you can do even better if you pursue call options rather than direct stock purchase. With options, you can get much better returns especially if you know for sure that a stock's price is going to rise. Let us examine the trade of a call option for 100 Yahoo! Shares. Let us say that these have a strike price of $50 but this price has a one-month timeline.

The call option is priced at $2 per share so you will buy the rights to purchase 100 shares of Yahoo stock, YHOO. The strike price now is $50, but this price will expire after one month. It will cost you $2 * 100 shares = $200 to purchase this call option. At this point, you own the rights to buy 100 shares at $50. Now in about 1 month's time, the price rises as was expected from $50 per share to $60. When this happens, then your options are said to be "In the Money."

If you are to sell this call option, you will sell it for $1000. This earns you a cool $800 profit. This is a 400% return on investment which you cannot make buying and selling shares. Now recall earlier when we spent $5000 buying shares. In this new scenario, we can spend the same amount of money buying options. $5000/$200 = 25 call options. If each option earns you $800 then 25 call options will earn you 25 * $800 = $20,000. This is an impressive return on investment and you can make huge profits this way. This is why call options are a far better choice than dealing directly in shares.

Different Scenarios

1. What if Stock does not Get to $60 but goes to $55

Remember that our stock, YHOO was worth $50 a share when we bought the call options. Now, what happens if, after the expiration of the time duration, the price does not hit $60 as was desired but goes up to only $55? Then you still win because the option is "In the Money." The stocks still gain an increase of $5 which works in your favor. If you wish, you can exercise your right to purchase the shares at the strike price and then sell them off at the stock market. You will then make a profit of $5 per share which adds up to, $5 * 100 = $500. A neat $500 profit for a single trade is not bad at all.

2. What if the price falls to $40 or below?

There are two other scenarios that are possible in this case. One is that there is no price movement at all. Let us assume that the price drops to $40 or below. You will have no desire to purchase the shares because they are available at the market at a cheaper price. In this instance, your options become worthless. You will not be able to claim any money and will have suffered a loss. In this case, your options will be considered as being "out of the money." You will also lose the initial amount you used to pay for the options.

What are the Profit and Loss Implications?

One thing worth noting when it comes to options is that you stand to gain big profits but your losses are only limited to the cost of the options no matter the size of the trade. In our case above, the maximum loss that was at risk was $200 while the best possible profit was about $20,000. In future, you may want to buy LEAPs options which are long-term options whose expiry dates are at least 1 year.

Call Options versus Put Options: What is the Difference?

It is important to understand the difference between call options and put options. Basically, call options give you a buying right. If you buy the option, then you have the right to buy any underlying stocks within a certain pre-defined time period. However, this is a right and not an obligation.

On the other hand, a put option is an option that grants you rights to sell an option at a set price and within a stipulated time period. You can choose to sell the put option if the price is right or exercise your right and buy the shares.

You have now learned more about trading options and how much more profitable they can be compared to investing in ordinary stocks. If you work hard, practice often and try to improve your techniques, then you will definitely be able to successfully trade and become profitable in the long run.

Chapter 5:
Some Simple Options Trading Strategies

O ptions trading features a wide variety of trading styles. They range from the basic, one-legged trades to the complex, multi-legged trades. The best part is that all strategies are based on two basic types. These are call options and put options. As a beginner, you should focus on learning one or two basic styles of trading. Once you master these styles adequately, you can then consider expanding your knowledge.

1. The Long Call

This strategy is very simple and pretty basic. It is ideal for beginners. Basically, as a trader, you find a call option and purchase it. This is known as going long. When you buy this option, you are doing so in the hope that the value of the underlying security will go up past the strike price within a given timeframe.

Example: Let us assume that a stock, ABC is trading at $50. Let us also assume that an options call is available at $5 per share for a period of 6 months. Like all others, this option contract is for 100 shares. This means that it will cost you or any other trader $5 * 100 = $500 for the contract.

Possible Outcomes

Now if everything works out as planned, then the possibilities or chances of striking it big are limitless. All that you need to hope for is for the price to move upwards. If the stock price hits the $100 mark, then your possible earnings could top $4,500. The linear progression of this kind of trade is limitless. The worst that could happen is you could lose the premium you paid for the contract. In this instance, you could lose $500.

You should use this strategy if your opinion is that the risk is worth the reward. In this case, the risk is pretty low and the rewards are potentially very impressive. It also saves you the hustle of actually buying the stock while still ensuring you benefit from them.

2. The Long Pull

Another very popular and very basic strategy is known as the Long Pull. This strategy is almost similar to the long call. The only difference here is that you will be rooting for a price fall of the underlying stock. A drop in price will put you in a better position to have the outcome that you desire.

Practical Example

Let us assume that ABC stock is at a price of $50. Now someone puts up a $50 put option. Each costs $5 and limited in time to a 6-month period. So if you were to buy a contract for 100 shares at $5 * 100 = $500. With this trade, you stand to benefit the most if the price drops to zero. Should this happen, then you will stand to make at least $5,000. On the other hand, the downside is that you will lose the premium you paid to acquire the stocks. In our case, this is $500.

Other Strategies

There are a number of other strategies that you can use. They include the covered call, the married put, and the short put. Here they are in brief:

The short put: This kind of trade is the direct opposite of the long put. Traders will sell their put or go short. The thinking or reasoning here is that the price of the stock will go up or remain stagnant until expiration. The pay off of a short put is the exact opposite of a long put.

Success Stories of Real-Life Options Traders

There are plenty of successful options traders out there. Many of them are well-educated and experts after trading for years and sometimes even decades. They serve to provide great examples to aspiring traders, beginners, and novices. Here is a look at some of these successful options traders.

1. Steven Place

Steven Place is a successful and respected options trader. Steven started out as an engineer working full-time in the corporate world. He was happy at his job but when the markets crashed in 2008, he decided to quit his job and become a full-time options trader. He has been trading options for the last 10 years or so and has become very successful.

According to Steven, trading has helped him unleash his full potential and earn so much more in his trades. He is able to trade with fewer risks and earn so much more. Steven also found out that he did not have to become a renowned guru or respected investor like Warren Buffet. Since he loved trading so much, it came naturally to him. He managed to convince his friends and family to raise funds and seriously begin trading.

Today, he is a rich and successful trader, a blogger, stock trade trainer, and so much more. He has a list of clients that he attends to regularly and also runs his blog and a website at http://www.investingwithoptions.com.

2. Jared Woodward

Another successful options trader is Jared Woodward. He was born and raised in Cannon Falls, Minnesota and graduated college with a finance degree. After college, he worked in the medical field for many years.

In 2014, he decided to quit his job and begin trading options. He started working as a financial adviser and in the process started to encourage and advise clients who expressed an interest in investing or trading.

Today, Jared is among the well-known, rich, successful, and resourceful options investors in Minnesota. He has managed to enter the field of finance and make a fortune for himself. He has also decided to pass on his knowledge to his clients. You can find him through his website, www.advancedfin.com, and engage him if you need assistance or advice. He is always happy to guide other traders, especially newbies and novice traders.

Conclusion

Thank you for making it through to the end of this book, let's hope it was informative and able to provide you with all of the tools you need to achieve your goals whatever they may be.

The next step is to apply the knowledge you acquire through this book to begin trading and profit from options. There are plenty of successful individuals who have turned their fortunes around and become successful, wealthy investors. You too can turn your fortunes around if you apply the knowledge and skills carefully described in this book.

Remember to start small and grow gradually. Implement the strategy that you are most conversant with and you will definitely perform well. Once you become good with one strategy, try and learn another one. The returns possible through options trading are much better compared to trading individual stocks.

Finally, if you found this book useful in any way, a review on Amazon is always appreciated!